45 P

GREAT ARTISTS COLLECTION

Five centuries of great art in full colour

RUBENS

by ᵹ*ENNIFER FLETCHER*

ENCYCLOPAEDIA BRITANNICA : LONDON

Volume ten

COVER: Detail from *Hélène Fourment with two of her Children* (Plate 45)

© *1968 by Phaidon Press Limited, London*

This revised edition published in 1972
by Encyclopaedia Britannica International Limited, London

ISBN 0 85229 110 8

Printed in Great Britain

RUBENS

Today Rubens is often admired but rarely liked; whereas in his own lifetime he was famous, fashionable and commercially successful. His intelligence extended beyond his art. He was sociable and articulate: hundreds of letters give evidence of his opinions, taste and commissions. We know far more about Rubens than we do about Rembrandt; and yet Rubens' life, with its contrasts between domestic tranquillity and international diplomacy, has somehow failed to capture the popular imagination. The circumstances of his life have been too crudely related to his art and have failed to illuminate his attitude to painting. In point of fact, Rubens has always been a little 'suspect', and is nowadays often accused of insincerity and vulgarity. His very brilliance and the incredible speed and ease with which he worked seem less impressive to the twentieth century than they did to contemporaries.

There are other barriers to an uninhibited appreciation of Rubens' art. Rubens was a devout Catholic who often painted for propagandist religious orders, such as the Jesuits, and most people reading this book will be deeply conditioned by Protestant traditions. His vision of female beauty is remote from contemporary ideals. He frequently used difficult symbols and allegorical figures whose meaning, though apparent to his contemporaries, we now have to look up in books. Today we tend to sympathise more easily with painters, like Rembrandt, whose work was not, in fact, always in accord with seventeenth-century assumptions about art. We like the idea of struggle, isolation and introversion. Not one of Rubens' many letters gives any hint of neurosis or of a creative crisis. It is disconcerting to find an artist openly boasting as Rubens did in a letter of 1621: 'My talents are such that I have never lacked courage to undertake any design, however vast in size or diversified in subject.' It is not comfortable to listen to Rubens as he advertises his own work, recommending his paintings and whetting his patron's appetite with promises of 'many beautiful nudes'.

Such objections to Rubens should not be casually swept aside. We have to admit that this is an artist who enjoyed painting rapes and naked women; and if we examine seventeenth-century reactions we find that in England, for example, there was some doubt about the tone of the mythological paintings that Rubens might produce for the Queen's bedroom at Greenwich. The agent in charge of this commission was instructed to see that the painter did not produce 'drunken-headed imaginary Gods'. A quick look at the Dresden *Bacchanal*, which is no Renaissance study in Dionysian ecstasy but a brutal description of physical incapacity, shows us exactly what they had to fear.

There are many different levels in both Rubens' standards and accomplishments. A painter working on such a scale and under such pressures could not always bring his deepest concentration to the work in hand. Rubens also accepted the seventeenth-century belief in a strict hierarchy of subject matter: it was better to paint Christ taking his supper at Emmaus than a group of peasants drinking in an inn. If we read Rubens' letters carefully, it will become clear that he went even further. The fact that a subject came from the Bible did not necessarily entitle it to elaborate and reverential treatment. An episode such as Abraham dismissing Hagar was to Rubens rather trivial and therefore suitable for a small scale panel painting. A *Bathsheba* (Plate 44) was obviously not meant to be worshipped in a church; it was a collector's piece, an Old Testament Venus at her bath, an open invitation to erotic thoughts. Here Rubens is different from Rembrandt for he works within traditional subject matter. Rembrandt was interested in visualising obscure and previously unillustrated Biblical subjects. But then Rembrandt lived in a country where church walls had been whitewashed and the market for religious art had violently contracted. Rubens accepted the expectations of patrons whose tastes had been influenced by sixteenth-century Venetian painting through conscious quotation. He will remind them that a Veronese, a Tintoretto or a Titian lies behind his own rendering of a subject.

It is comparatively easy to become involved in a single painting by Rembrandt, but many people, even though they easily recognise Rubens' style of painting, find it difficult to recall individual pictures by him. They acquire a generalised conception of his work, a glorious amalgam of martyred saints and riotous bacchanals. But in doing so, without probing deeper, the layman misses one of the most exciting aspects of Rubens' life and art. He will not perceive the painter's brilliant stage management of his opportunities, or see him limbering up like an athlete, sometimes holding himself in reserve, even turning down commissions that he felt were beneath his capability or would typecast him in the wrong role. Rubens' sense of his own destiny, his unshakable belief in his own power and in the originality of his own way of applying paint cannot be ignored if we are to understand his paintings fully. In the same way, we should try to accept, frankly, Rubens' aesthetic self-consciousness. We can meditate with a Rembrandt prophet, we are drawn into the stillness and our visual reactions grow slowly almost as if in harmony with the rate the picture itself grew. After a time we can almost forget that we are looking at a picture at all. But when we study a Rubens Madonna ascending to heaven (Plate 7), we sense Rubens at work, making the picture. The way he has visualised the scene may be powerful and impressive, but we only temporarily believe that it could happen that way. The movement in his paintings prevents contemplation; it is hard to get lost in the event. With Rubens, we are always aware of Art.

This was intentional. Rubens' art was consciously derived from works of the Italian sixteenth century, and the more we know about sixteenth-century art the better will we appreciate his achievement. Rubens will paint a 'Fine Art' *Assumption* which should remind us of other great *Assumptions* by Titian and Annibale Carracci. It is not just a picture of the Virgin going up to heaven, a brilliant illusion of a momentary revelation, it is Rubens showing us that he can out-paint the Italians at their own game. This is deliberate incantation. The Madonna is magnified by technical virtuosity. It is not easy to disentangle the glory of Rubens from the glory of God. Pure technical skill, however, is constantly under-valued in this century and Rubens' type of excitable, elevated, self-generating, self-conscious creativity is not prized, as it should be. In literature, Milton has already fallen to the axe for comparable reasons.

Rubens has remained a painter's painter, and artists have made the most perceptive criticisms of his work. His art, so rich in quotation, has bred great painting in its turn. Rubens has shown a few artists what to paint, but to the majority he has revealed a way of applying paint and harmonising colours. Rubens is the great undenominational painter and his work has been accessible to artists of different nationalities, temperaments and interests. A study of Rubens can serve as a brilliant introduction to Baroque art but it can do more than this. It can teach us to think outside the limitations of centuries and it can lead us to reconsider the innumerable ways in which one artist can influence another. Artists have found Rubens' work relatively easy to break down. In using Rubens they have not felt themselves totally committed to a certain taste or dogma. Rubens, like Titian, is open to highly fruitful misinterpretations.

Rubens can, and has been, referred to on many different levels. His work helped Renoir achieve the pearly flesh tones of his *Grandes Baigneuses*. Watteau copied several of his chalk drawings and studied the Marie de' Medici cycle (Plate 18) attentively. Constable lectured on his landscapes at Hampstead. Cézanne made drawings from the Marie de' Medici cycle, and Kokoschka was able to study Rubens *modelli* when painting a ceiling in a London house which contains a large collection of Rubens' work. If we know nothing about Rubens, we cannot hope to understand Delacroix, who, quite consciously and somewhat emotionally, pitched his art in a Rubensian key. Delacroix saw Rubens as the Romantic hero, the anti-academic, the genius who could break the rules. Delacroix is one of the few artists to gain an overall view of Rubens' career and perhaps only he has really tried to define Rubens' originality. He admired his power of conveying energy and feeling, of controlling visibility and commanding a response over vast architectural spaces. He saw that Rubens' colour was not purely 'scientific' in application, used only to record optical facts, but that it was also a means of conveying emotion. Delacroix's art grew out of Rubens and he needed Rubens' skills and fluency. He studied many of the paintings reproduced in this book, copying the *Rape of the Daughters of Leucippus* (Plate 15), the *Battle of the Amazons* (Plate 13) and the *Reception of Marie de' Medici* (Plate 18). In his journal he struggled to describe the nature of his own response to Rubens' work. He tried to describe his sense of shock and rapture and he rightly connected it with the Michelangelesque scale, *terribilità* and distortion in Rubens' art.

We can learn a lot about twentieth-century attitudes to Rubens just by considering the plates selected for this book. There are a high proportion of coloured sketches and paintings made by Rubens for himself. In this century we have placed great emphasis on creativity, improvisation and the whole process of making a picture, *as a private act*, in which feeling is of more account than intelligence. But even though this makes it very hard to see Rubens as contemporaries saw him, his work is so rich and varied that it can happily support more than one interpretation, and provide an infinite variety of pleasure. Rubens will interest those who believe that paint should have an exciting texture, that it can be beautiful in itself and that it should not hide behind the objects that it describes. They will admire Rubens' ability to animate a large surface, to use the colour of the wood panel as a unifying factor, to turn nude forms fluently in and out of space, and to distort forms in the direction of an overall rhythm. In a curious way a Rubens can stand not only as a beautiful picture but also as an attractive idea. Rubens will remain part of many people's private mythology, for we still need giants and genius figures, artists who will constantly remind us of the complexity of art and of the limitations of language when applied to it. He is a very 'visual' artist, who makes his effect on our seeing rather than our thinking, a man who has been able to paint certain surfaces so satisfactorily, and realised them so completely, that it is now hard to see real flesh or a real sunset except in his terms. As long as Rubens' paintings are attacked with razors, as long as his nudes disappear from library books, we can rest assured that a large part of his message is still 'getting through'.

One of the main problems that confronts anyone who studies Rubens is the sheer size of his output. For this reason, it is easier to come to grips with his art by considering various isolated aspects.

Rubens and the antique

In the seventeenth century most artists drew from classical sculpture or from casts; it was part of an orthodox art training, since classical sculpture still retained the authority which it had exercised over artists of the High Renaissance. By looking at classical art, a young artist learnt to reproduce a certain selection of idealised types, forms, contours and gestures. Art theory still leaned heavily on Aristotle's *Poetics* and Plato's conception of ideal form. Great art was a kind of frozen theatre; the artist's figures were actors, they relayed a dramatic story through dignified gestures and suitably noble expressions. Study of classical art was supposed to teach one how to do this well, and young artists were advised to work from the antique until they had learnt to see life in terms of classical prototypes. A sculptor like Bernini was proud to admit that in his youth, when in difficulties with a statue, he had gone to the classical figure of Antinous 'as to the oracle'. This statue of a nude youth, in the Vatican gallery where it was also studied by Rubens, was then considered to be one of the most important statues of antiquity. Poussin firmly believed in 'those fine old Greeks, who invented everything that is beautiful', and Caravaggio was criticised for challenging the superiority of classical art and for suggesting that flowers were as hard to paint as human beings.

Rubens' position was rather complex, since he was less dogmatic, less convinced of the benefits to be derived from the study of classical art than most of his contemporaries. In an essay that he wrote on the use of classical sculpture he explained that while it was good for some artists it was so harmful to others 'as to destroy their art'. In other words what might be good for Rubens might not be so good for someone else. It is worth remembering that Van Dyck, Rubens' most brilliant pupil, found Rome uncongenial and was constitutionally uninterested in the antique. We must remember that Rubens had an eye for good painting, almost irrespective of its style; he judged pictures on how they looked, not on the quality of the ideas that lay behind them. Rubens admired Caravaggio and copied from Michelangelo, and he owned Elsheimers as well as Titians. He could re-use the figure of God from the Sistine Ceiling or a peasant from Bruegel. He never concealed his own empiricism or subjectivity. He had preferences for certain kinds of classical work and clear ideas on quality. He could extract information on armour or iconography from a Roman relief but this did not mean that he found it beautiful or stylistically sympathetic. Unlike Poussin, he never fell in love with the clarity, the stiffness or the actual archaic qualities of certain reliefs. Rubens was not temperamentally addicted to order; he did not 'flee confusion as day the night'; rather, he revelled in the energy and confused movement of the great battle sarcophagi.

The difference between Rubens' and Poussin's response is made clear in their reaction to a book written by Francis Junius containing descriptions of the lost paintings of antiquity. Poussin was very enthusiastic and was stimulated by it to elaborate his theory of the Modes; but Rubens qualified his praise. He suggested to the author that it might have been more useful to describe works of art by modern Italian painters for these paintings still existed: 'one might point to them with the finger and say "there they are". Those things which are perceived by the senses produce a sharper and more durable impression, require a closer examination and afford richer material for study than those which present themselves to us only in the imagination.' Poussin could talk about judging pictures with reason rather than compulsion, but Rubens' art is aggressively seductive, sensual and full of unconcealed erotic appeal. Both Rubens and Poussin were very erudite but Rubens' intelligence seems more compartmentalised. His art grows out of visual stimuli: a naked backside, a Roman goddess or a Venetian canvas. Unlike Poussin, he could not work up his imagery from a philosophical idea; although an antiquarian, he had no special interest in classicism as a general concept. He did not deal in abstractions, he did not – as he said on the death of his first wife – feel that one could be equally indifferent to all things in this life. Rubens' rate of creativity was far faster than Poussin's and he needed constant stimuli, an ever expanding vocabulary of classical forms. He was interested in the tangible aspects of antiquity, in Roman history as well as in mythology. The esoteric had little appeal for him. He insisted that marble must be transformed into 'living flesh' and so most of the drawings after the antique are made with soft chalk. His whole art is directed to the animation of the surface.

Rubens shared his interest in surfaces with Bernini, who might even have been encouraged in his approach by Rubens' example. Both artists worked for Scipione Borghese and knew the sculpture in his collection. Both were attracted to large figure groups, to the *Farnese Bull* and the *Laocöon*, which so successfully evoked violent movement. The work of sixteenth-century artists like Michelangelo, whose style was to some extent grounded on them, appealed to Rubens and Bernini for similar reasons. Both were so involved with classical objects that they instinctively identified classical characters with particular classical statues. Hercules meant the *Farnese Hercules* (British Museum), while Apollo meant the statue in the Belvedere. Rubens' artistic aim was quite straightforward. He wanted to bring the world of the antique sarcophagi back to life, simply to make that world more plausible and three-dimensional. Any source that would help him became important. Rubens was not deeply interested in fifteenth-century art, but he copied Mantegna's *Triumph of Caesar* (London, National Gallery) because he felt that it contained authentic information on the appearance of a Roman Triumph.

Rubens could use a small-scale prototype for a giant-size picture; he could convert an Adonis into Christ, a Roman matron into a Christian saint. He had an exceptional visual memory, and figures originally copied from someone else soon become a natural part of his own visual vocabulary. We can sometimes recognise such borrowings when he 'thinks aloud' in his *modelli*, but on other occasions we fail to recognise them, so transformed are they by the personal rhythm of Rubens' brush-strokes. Rubens used words as well as images to stimulate his imagination. He couldn't restrain his joy when he discovered an uncut manuscript describing a classical orgy in a Spanish library. Sometimes, as he painted his scenes from Ovid or his Bacchanals, portions of the classical texts were read aloud to him in the original Latin.

It is not easy to set a limit on Rubens' debt to antiquity; it was never just a case of a year or two's culture in Italy. Antiquity and its history was part of his way of life; his private letters were larded with Roman proverbs, and mottoes from Seneca and Juvenal were carved above his doors; he was respected by the most scholarly antiquarians of his day. His house was full of classical sculpture. His son was trained to write essays on tripods, and his wife even used a light-weight classical porridge spoon when she was pregnant. His brother Phillip was an accomplished classical scholar and Rubens illustrated his books, and from this correspondence we can see Rubens learning through his eyes. Rubens' attitude to subject matter made several antiquarians look silly. He looked harder at objects than they and applied common sense to what he saw. It is amazing that Rubens was not weighed down by his own erudition but that erudition, like his technical fluency, seems to have been easily acquired.

Perhaps Rubens was saved from dryness by his interest in narrative, for even as a young man in Rome we can watch him trying to animate his sculptural models. He often drew from the same pieces, as his near contemporary Golzius, but unlike Golzius, he rarely tries to reproduce the sensation of marble. With Rubens it is almost as if he is already thinking of some context in which to use the figure. He will draw from unusual angles. He can disturb our preconceived conception of a figure by drawing it steeply foreshortened or by creeping around the back to take it from an unfamiliar, almost unrecognisable position. He shines a light on Michelangelo's *Battle of the Centaurs*, draws it once and then illuminates it from the other direction and draws it again, fascinated by the instability of appearances. In his letters he constantly apologises for his black and white drawings and will give loving descriptions of the flaws in the marble, of transitions in colour from whites to creams to browns. Like Bernini and Michelangelo, he recognised the emotional impact of violent foreshortening, and as with Guido Reni, his conception of physiognomical suffering was based on the upturned head of the father in the *Laocöon* group. This experience is behind his drawings for the Antwerp *Raising of the Cross*; it can be sensed in his oil sketch of two Apostles' heads from the Bromley-Davenport collection (Plate 27).

Rubens' idea of 'great art' was based on classical precepts and in *The Horrors of War* (London, National Gallery) he symbolises the death of art in a drawing of the Three Graces which is trampled underfoot by Mars the God of War. Perhaps we can best see Rubens' relationship to the antique by looking at a late painting of *The Three Graces* now in Madrid (Plate 48). Already by this date the subject had merged in Rubens' mind with the *Judgement of Paris*. The Graces were constantly represented in antiquity and to the seventeenth-century spectator the subject was charged with classical associations. Raphael had made the definitive High Renaissance comment on the theme. For Rubens this is a statement on the female form in triplicate. The classical origin is not so obvious, it is hardly a memory; but the women are built on the scale of the Venus de Milo, even though, at the same time, they are 'softened into living flesh'. Rubens wishes us to feel that this is 'nature not art'.

We see things that no one else has painted before, flesh which is loose enough to quiver and shake. We see creases under the arms, dimples around the base of the spine and indentations where the figures grasp each other. These details, observed from living models, are absorbed into the rhythm of the general contour. Rubens' eye, disciplined by the study of classical form, does not have to concentrate on one aspect, and is free to focus on another. He has re-directed his looking – but within the framework of classical art. The ancient meaning of the Graces, those who give and receive, is truly reinforced by Rubens' treatment. The Grace viewed from the back, so often a central accent in earlier designs, is now off-centre. It is difficult to separate the action which is, as it should be, completely reciprocal.

In his late work Rubens seems to be stressing the tangibility, pushing his illusion at us by forcing the painted figures to touch or to take hold. Chain movement and dancing become his ideal. Looking at this picture we see why Rubens cannot, like Rembrandt, paint deliberately anti-classical pictures. He will not search conscientiously for an alternative ideal although he will occasionally borrow one from someone else. His eye was 'elevated' early in Italy, where he saw classical art in its proper setting. The result is not as is so often implied a simple blend of northern realism and Italian idealism. It is more complex than that. A personal way of moving the brush, an astonishing response to complicated colour harmony, a personal attitude to the surface, an extraordinary visual memory – all these have produced something which is usually called typically Flemish. It is less clever but more honest to call it typically Rubens.

The diplomatic career

Had Rubens never touched a brush, had he never even seen a picture, many of us would have at least heard his name. The historians of this century would have been unable to resist him and we should have read of a certain Peter Paul Rubens, diplomat, in a Sunday review. In the National Gallery in London there is a small coloured sketch of *The Horrors of War*. The large picture which grew out of it was completed by 1638. It was probably made for Ferdinand de' Medici, the Grand Duke of Tuscany. It is not the kind of painting that art students copy, or many people stop to look at, and yet it deserves attention, for it is a denunciation of war. This work should show us to what degree Rubens' deep involvement in international politics in the 1620s influenced his handling of certain themes. The type of subject had meant a great deal to him. In 1635 he was involved in designing temporary triumphal arches which were to be erected in Antwerp to celebrate the visit of the Cardinal Archduke Ferdinand of Spain. Rubens' designs were not purely triumphal for they contained warnings on the economic crisis that had hit Antwerp since the blockading of the River Scheldt by the Dutch. Rubens painted Mercury, God of Trade, deserting the city. On another of the arches he suggested that war was imminent and painted Janus the Roman war god bursting out of his temple.

Rubens had been a top-ranking diplomat employed by Isabella, Regent of the Southern Netherlands. He had worked on briefs from Spain and his mission was to bring Holland back into the Spanish Catholic fold. It is interesting that Rubens, in contrast with the majority of diplomats, held fast to the completely unrealistic belief that Protestant Holland would surrender her independence. Rubens had close diplomatic and family contacts with a group of Dutch Catholics and through them he seems to have gained an entirely distorted view of the situation within Holland itself. Rubens threw himself into a strenuous diplomatic career only because he quite sincerely and deeply believed in the possibility of peace. When he was in London in 1630 he acted on his own initiative and made a private visit to the Dutch ambassador. Risking personal insult, he implored him to reopen negotiations. If he had been successful, he would not have retired from politics in that year. Rubens was used to seeing his art used as a pawn in a political game. Not far from his *Horrors of War*, in the National Gallery, is his picture illustrating the *Fruits of Peace*, which he presented to Charles I in 1630 to set the seal on the King's promise to pursue a policy of peaceful co-existence with Spain; a policy that Rubens and his employers thought would encourage the Dutch to do likewise.

Rubens explained the meaning of *The Horrors of War* in a letter that he sent to the Flemish painter Sustermans, who was to unpack the picture on its arrival in Florence. He explained that the woman in black is Europe ravished by war and stripped of her wealth. In the centre Venus, goddess of love, tries to hold back Mars, the god of war. Above them the classical Furies bring famine and disease. Architecture is represented by a man with compasses thrown down on the ground and Harmony is symbolised by the female musician with the lute. Now, Rubens is frequently charged with insincerity and many of the guides at the Pitti Gallery seem to think that this picture is an outsize excuse for the painting of nude figures. It is true that a twentieth-century spectator might be tempted to ask why Rubens doesn't give us a more documentary account of war, why he doesn't do it like Callot and show us troops looting and burning villages. Rubens' own letters contain vivid accounts of refugees struggling towards the Dutch frontier, of outbreaks of plague and dysentery, but we must remember that Rubens is a cosmopolitan artist and that his art, like Titian's, had an international circulation. Rubens' messages had to be understood in Protestant London and in Catholic Madrid and just as there was a special diplomatic language so there was a diplomatic style in painting. Allegory is the Latin, the international code, of seventeenth-century art and contemporary treatises on poetry extol it as the most important branch of literature. In the seventeenth century it becomes a primary means of expression. We are no longer used to elaborate images like the Ship of State. We do not think of good luck as did Rubens, who describes it in a letter as a 'woman turning her back'. Our thoughts do not easily freeze into figures and phrases like the 'Wind of Change' which crop up occasionally in political speeches. They are no longer a living part of our language. Rubens could not paint, like Bruegel, Dutch soldiers sacking a Belgian village because he did not wish to illustrate a particular historical war. He wanted to make a grandiose denunciation of all war. If we read Rubens' own letters we shall see him instinctively drawing on classical quotations when trying to describe personal emotion. If a friend dies he does not indulge in an account of his own sorrow but will choose to distance himself from the tragedy by finding an appropriate quotation from Horace to cover the event.

Diplomacy involves constant compromise and Rubens knew what this meant in terms of painting. He was only able to do justice to the rather inglorious episodes in the life of the French Queen Mother, Marie de' Medici, because he firmly believed in the Divine Right of all kings and could sincerely make direct visual comparisons between her birth and Christ's nativity, her marriage and that of Joseph and Mary. Rubens was well aware that the commentator who showed this series to Marie's son, Louis XIII, had to change and conceal the true meaning of the pictures 'with great skill'. Rubens felt that the whole cycle would have caused less embarrassment had he been left to arrange the subjects himself. We must remember that Rubens the artist suffered at the hands of Rubens the diplomat. His support and reception of the exiled Marie de' Medici led to a temporary ban on Rubens' engravings in France and meant the end of his plans to decorate another gallery in the Luxembourg palace with paintings depicting the reign of her husband Henry IV. In his own *Horrors of War* Rubens has evolved a personal commentary on the situation. War affects culture for it can destroy literature, painting, music and architecture. Rubens the diplomat failed to negotiate a peace and Rubens the artist might have to pay for that failure. Picasso could do nothing about the planes that bombed Guernica but Rubens is painting something that he feels partly responsible for. His letter to Sustermans ends with an illuminating postscript. With rather uncharacteristic but perhaps significant humility, Rubens tells this mediocre artist that should the picture be damaged or should the artist not find everything to his satisfaction he has Rubens' permission to retouch the work.

It is of course hard to prove that Rubens' personal involvement in international affairs deepened his conception of allegory but this picture shows us how Rubens can enliven allegory, how he can impose on it all the passion of a mythological episode. Rubens' diplomatic career did enrich his art in a very direct way for it gave him continual opportunities to study the important Venetian paintings and the great European collections. We should remember that the buyer of *The Horrors of War* was educated on Venetian art and that he might respond more immediately than we do to the implications in the figures. To him the Venus who hangs on to Mars could be related to that Venus, in Titian's painting, who tries to restrain the young Adonis before the hunt. We should realise how appropriate it is that Rubens, the second great international artist, should follow so closely the solutions of the first. The meaning of this picture is reinforced in every colour and in every form. Europe is not just a fat woman about to fall. She is a tottering, unstable, crow-like shape doomed by her attributes and also by her black. Conflict is actually physically there in the picture, in the two clashing reds that rip across the centre of the painting.

Society portraits

When Rubens was painting portraits, weddings could still be made by proxy and a portrait could still make or break a marriage. Portraits were a part of politics; in the sixteenth century the Venetian Senate had voted to offer Titian's services to would-be allies. In the seventeenth century, portraits were still taken very literally and they often acted as a real substitute for an absent king or general. Travelling fast from Court to Court, portraits were important taste-makers and trend-setters, often compared, frequently exchanged and nearly always talked about. Patrons learnt about art more easily through their own portraits than by studying subject pictures, for they felt freer to criticise a likeness than to question the principles underlying the composition of a history painting. This led to a curious situation. In seventeenth-century theory, portraiture came low down in the hierarchy of subject matter but in practice a skilful portrait painter was all-powerful, since he was concerned not only with a record of a face but also with an elaborate comment on his sitter's social status. In making this statement, a portrait painter of talent might also manage to imply much about the degree of social distance between his patron and himself.

When Rubens arrived in Italy, at the beginning of the seventeenth century, Flemish portrait specialists (like his Mantuan colleague, Pourbus) were the acknowledged experts, earning high salaries at the Italian Courts. Rubens wrote very little about portraiture, but there is evidence to show that, initially, he was afraid of being confined to a narrow career as a court portraitist. In 1603, he actually refused to paint a series of French Court beauties for his patron, the Duke of Mantua. A pin-up set of anonymous French courtesans was unworthy of his time and talent – although an opportunity to paint an influential patron, the politically powerful Duke of Lerma, or the wife of a leading member of the Genoese nobility was quite another matter.

The Genoese aristocracy was notoriously proud. With Brigida Spinola-Doria (Plate 1), Rubens was also painting a sitter whose family owned paintings by Titian. He was to meet this situation again and again. Conscious of the fact that his portraits would hang beside great examples of sixteenth-century portraiture, he made a point of studying the sources of the international portrait style, copying the head from Titian's equestrian portrait of Charles V, and Raphael's Baldassare Castiglione. In the glamorous portrait of Brigida Spinola-Doria, Rubens tried to achieve a sense of social distinction by means of imposing architectural details. Brigida is part of the palace in which she hangs. In the seventeenth century portraits were not always painted from the life. Many artists did not even see their sitters, and were asked to base their likeness on older pictures. Patrons became bored with long sittings, and artists had to be content with an hour or two at a time. Rubens had probably one or two short sittings in which he made detailed drawings of heads and hands and a more rapid compositional sketch with notes on colour and costume. Patrons expected an elaborate account of their clothing, and an artist often found himself painting clothes which had been specially ordered for a portrait, and which were worn by a model or draped on a lay-figure. The artist could not invent, he was expected to be accurate, with the result that costumes can now be reconstructed completely from the evidence supplied by portraits. Patrons were preconditioned to expect a certain range of gestures and a certain type of setting and might not take kindly to drastic innovations. The Doria portrait, however, is quietly remarkable in that Brigida, unlike the ladies in paintings by Mor and Pourbus, does not ostentatiously finger a crucifix or pendant; nor does she support herself against a table top. The impression is not of a portrait pose but of a figure only momentarily at rest; she has stopped to look at us and will soon move on.

In this picture we are presented with the sitter, as it were, in close-up. And unlike the women in many society portraits of the time, Brigida is allowed a personality, she responds to the spectator and is about to smile. She wears her elaborate costume easily and naturally. Its details are not laid stiffly across the surface – as in an English Elizabethan portrait – but are everywhere related to the human body beneath. But then Rubens was always able to combine a sense of detail and surface texture with a feeling for the underlying structure of a form; and we can see how he simultaneously controls all parts of his portraits if we look at his unfinished picture of the Duchess of Buckingham at Dulwich.

When we look at Rubens' portraits of women we should remember that changes in fashion can condition an artist's choice of viewpoint and his selection of forms. A huge ruff was very difficult to handle for it could so easily lead to the isolation of the head from the body. In the Doria portrait its slant is echoed in the angle of the crimson drapery above, and against this slightly exaggerated angle the turn of the head and the displaced necklace underline the impression of a sitter confronting an audience. Rubens' Genoese portraits provided a brilliant starting point for Van Dyck but the picture of Brigida Spinola-Doria is also prophetic of Rubens' later work: in it he has hit upon his ideal female expression. Critics have frequently pointed out that all Rubens' women look remarkably alike. This is a roundabout way of admitting a simple fact. A man will often feel a genuine compulsion to reproduce his own particular feminine ideal. In Rubens' case it is not only an ideal appearance but an ideal response. Rubens' women are united by their smile; and this can be hesitant, openly provocative or purely sociable. Rubens' approach to Court portraiture differed radically from that of Van Dyck. Van Dyck was temperamentally addicted to high society while Rubens deliberately chose not to live at Court or to marry into the nobility. Van Dyck seems to have identified himself with the social aspirations of his sitters while Rubens' exhausting diplomatic career left him with a healthy respect for certain outstanding individuals but a rather jaded view of the whole social group. Both Rubens and Van Dyck accepted the courtier's right to visual magnification but both worked with different forms of flattery. If Rubens intends to flatter he does so very openly. A woman's mouth can be minute while her eyes can be huge.

The Duke of Buckingham, whose likeness is preserved in numerous portraits by Honthorst, Cornelius Jonson and Mytens, was famous for his languid, rather effeminate beauty but Rubens chose to celebrate his power through a feat of equestrian mastery and by inbuilt allusions to his career as Commander of the Navy, and Governor of Dover Castle. In this now lost picture we can see an important stylistic connection between Rubens' portraits and his other commissions. The Buckingham is an expanded portrait, a picture that is growing into a history painting. Rubens employs all those tricks that he had learnt while working on his recently completed *Marie de' Medici* cycle. We feel Rubens angling the commission in the direction of his own interests, and it could be argued that the naked sea gods are too obtrusive. This portrait makes us realise how difficult it is to strike an exact balance between the idea that glorified and the details that identify the man – a dichotomy that is at the heart of seventeenth-century portraiture.

Rubens' best portraits are of sitters whom he knew well and whose intellectual interests he shared. When he painted male friends like Nonnius, a Doctor of Medicine, he concentrated on a speaking likeness, on creating an impression of instantaneous movement (Plates 22 and 24). Nonnius, like Rembrandt's Doctor Anslo and Bernini's Scipione Borghese, addresses an audience. He is inviting us to argue. His book falls out of the picture towards us but tantalisingly we are not allowed to read his text. In this portrait the sitter's head is relatively small but our attention is drawn irresistibly towards it by the large bust of Hippocrates, the hero of classical medicine, on one side and the shelf of reference books on the other. The marble bust, as so often in Rubens, is painted softly; it is over-animated and we are made to see a strong visual simile between the bust, displaced from its niche, and the head of the living doctor, the modern incarnation of the antique ideal that has taken its place.

In the sixteenth century collectors amused themselves by projecting family likenesses into their favourite busts of Roman emperors, and in the seventeenth century this idea seems to have been taken even more literally. Artists like Bernini even went so far as to adjust a sitter's features in favour of a classical prototype. Since Louis XIV was often compared to Alexander the Great, why shouldn't he also be made a little like Alexander? Hélène Fourment, in contemporary costume, sitting in a modern armchair (Plate 28), has a face which is far less Venus-like in its proportions than that of Hélène Fourment half-naked wrapped up in a fur coat (Plate 30). Seventeenth-century portraits are far more specific than those painted in the sixteenth century. We can measure the difference in approach by comparing Rubens' copy of Raphael's *Castiglione* with the original. Looking at the Raphael, it is hard to gauge the sitter's state of mind; while in Rubens' version he looks frankly worried. High Renaissance repose, simplification and intuitive symmetry, have broken down and been transformed into an emotional, Baroque statement. The sixteenth-century head looks almost blank beside the seventeenth-century painting. The force of the feeling has spilled over into the background: the head is haloed in light and the once smooth contour has become agitated, discontinuous and jagged.

Looking again at the Nonnius we see that Rubens is the master of externalised feeling. His physiognomic range is far narrower than Rembrandt's for he is mainly interested in social expressions, in what can be seen rather than in what can only be implied. The Nonnius bears all the hall-marks of the Rubensian treatment: the nostrils – that moving breathing part of the face that becomes so important in seventeenth-century portraiture – are enlarged and painted as though seen slightly from below. Typical of Rubens are the double scarlet lines that rim the eye, the echoing of the shape of the ear in the rhythm of the swirling hair, and the overstrong highlight on the nose. In this portrait Rubens has rejected completely the Renaissance ideal of balancing halves, of unity acquired by repetition of evenly measured units, and even the idea of a neutral flesh tint. Instead, each feature is rhythmically connected to the next by curving strokes and lines. If we compare a portrait like this with one by Van Dyck, whose portraiture was based on Rubens' example, we shall immediately see startling differences. In Van Dyck's picture of Cornelius van der Geest (London, National Gallery) the Rubensian red line has been replaced by a trail of liquid white. The brush-strokes are still visible in the face, but they are slacker and spread out more independently over the surface. There is a suggestion of indulgence in an overall pattern for its own sake, whereas Rubens allows the strokes to follow more exactly the contours of the forms. The result is a vital intellectual Nonnius and a pensive melancholy van der Geest. Each artist achieves his own ideal expression, which grows quite naturally out of an instinctive, highly personal form of pictorial calligraphy.

Family portraits

Rubens was not obsessively interested in his own appearance. His self-portraits are straightforward, and they are devoid of that narcissistic element that is so disturbing in the self-portraits by the young Van Dyck. Unlike Rembrandt, Rubens did not use his own features as a basis for studies in physiognomic expression. When he paints himself, it is usually to document some significant event in his life, or in response to a request from an important patron. In 1623, for example, Rubens was commissioned to paint a self-portrait that was presented to the future Charles I, then Prince of Wales (now at Windsor Castle). In the seventeenth century the rising social status of artists is reflected in a general increase in fancy self-portraits and the subject of several paintings becomes the creative act itself. In *Las Meninas*, Velazquez painted himself at work on a group portrait surrounded by those courtiers and dwarfs who had provided the raw material for so much of his life's work; in several portraits, Rembrandt depicts himself brush in hand; even Vermeer allows us to look over the shoulder of an artist painting from his model. Rubens never paints himself as an artist, but always as a gentleman, enjoying the status that he had achieved by virtue of his artistic talent (Plates 5 and 29).

In 1609, when he had just accepted the post of Painter to the Court in Brussels, and at a time when he had committed himself to a future involving much official imagery, he produced one of the greatest autobiographical pictures of the seventeenth century. He painted himself and his new wife Isabella Brant sitting beneath a honeysuckle arbour (Plate 5). In this portrait, Rubens was bent upon finding a pictorial solution that could be completely dissociated from the formality of court portraiture; one that could contain his personal feelings; and yet one in which those feelings could be publicised and magnified by traditional associations with the theme of love.

In working out his design and conception, Rubens was influenced by representations of courtly gardens of love, a vernacular theme common in sixteenth-century Flemish art. He set the scene for his own marriage-portrait in the context of aristocratic relaxation, and his picture becomes a great close-up, a brilliantly expanded detail from one of these garden scenes. In this particular context, Rubens' floral symbolism and the almost archaic gesture of the finger pointing to Isabella's ring do not seem out of place. Like the aristocrats who play in these gardens, Rubens and Isabella Brant are dressed in the most fashionable and expensive clothes. This element might have been difficult to control, and the painting could so easily have degenerated into an ostentatious fashion-plate, but Rubens avoids this pitfall through brilliant 'cutting'. Isabella's 'humility' position on the ground is counter-balanced by the height of her tall hat, but Rubens avoids a repetition of this form by cutting off his own hat just above the brim.

This is a picture with a meaning and the idea of unity in marriage is built into the composition. The external contours of the forms are swept into the circular movement of the design. Isabella's arm rhymes visually with Rubens' leg; his foot is covered by her dress and the close physical association of these parts is echoed, at the very centre of the painting, in the way her hand is placed gently on the top of her husband's. This interrelationship of forms is reinforced by the colour. The two figures are dressed to match, and here we feel that Rubens has indulged in the glory of individual colours for their own sake. The plums, blacks, orange and blue are allowed an independent visual status, and are not swept into those swift relationships of broken tone that are so common a feature of the later paintings, and which are largely achieved by the visible direction of Rubens' brush-stroke. This painting is complex in another way as well. Few self-portraits, surely, have ever been so successfully camouflaged. There is none of the awkward angling of the head so often visible in pictures artists paint of themselves. Rubens looks out as though he were confronting some anonymous portrait painter, and it is only by accident that we know that he is facing himself.

In 1630 Rubens married Hélène Fourment, a silk merchant's daughter. She was related to his first wife and was only sixteen. Rubens was well over fifty and in a letter to a friend confessed that he was tired of celibacy. He points out that he could have married a lady of the court but had deliberately chosen a middle-class wife, 'one who would not blush to see me take my brushes in my hand'. Whilst it would be too crude to suppose that Rubens married for a model it is true that he became visually infatuated with his new wife, who enjoyed a contemporary reputation as a great beauty. Hélène Fourment's face and body recur in all categories of his art. She became an all-pervading common denominator in his work, and around her features the middle-aged artist was able to generate new fantasies. Rubens had retired from his diplomatic career and had begun to paint more and more for his own pleasure. He had always enjoyed painting his children and had frequently used them as models for cupids and cherubim. He painted them in very much the same spirit as a modern father might constantly re-photograph his children. In the Munich portrait of Hélène Fourment, and again in the Louvre picture (Plate 45), he produced frankly appealing, almost sentimental paintings.

On his death, Rubens left his wife a painting, a portrait of herself in the nude draped in a fur coat (Plate 30). Art historians have been unnecessarily pedantic about this picture. Does it really matter if she is a Venus or a Bathsheba, whether she has just taken or is about to have a bath? Whilst we must admit that Rubens had a certain range of associations hovering in his mind, these need not necessarily have been settled on any one specific subject. When Rubens paints a Venus or Bathsheba he usually leaves us in no doubt of the fact. Rubens' preliminary drawing for the painting shows Hélène sitting down and the uncharacteristic, though not unbeautiful lengthening of her legs in the painting may indicate a certain amount of hesitancy on the artist's part as to the final pictorial identity of the figure. Rubens sees Hélène Fourment through memories of Titian's *Girl with a Fur* (Vienna), of which he had made a replica, and which in the seventeenth century was thought of as an image of a prostitute or mistress. It may be significant that he had it at the back of his mind when producing his own portrait of his favourite model. Rembrandt had followed a very similar procedure when he painted his wife, Saskia, as the goddess of flowers after seeing Titian's *Flora* in Amsterdam. Rubens could think of Hélène in many different roles and it is only in his paintings of her that he really exposes himself. During his diplomatic career Rubens had often been snubbed and insulted by aristocrats. In 1630 he had failed to gain the post of envoy to the court in London because it was claimed that he 'practised an art and lived by the product of his work'. It is, therefore, interesting to see him in the Munich 'wedding-portrait' of this time (Plates 25 and 28) representing his middle-class wife with all the glory of the court-portrait formula. We have the armchair pose, the magnificent costume, the columns and curtains, all those ingredients which he combined in his early Genoese portraits of the seated Brigida Spinola-Doria. But in the Munich picture the whole mechanism is turned inside out and our preconceived ideas of decorum are destroyed. The strict relationship between the figure and its setting is broken: the armchair is tilted and the life of the figure throbs into the background. The violets, silvers and blacks sparkle like anthracite; the curtain behind Hélène is arbitrarily dissolved, and gives way to an evocation of moving clouds and open air.

We should now look from the face of Hélène in her sumptuous dress (Plate 28) to the Hélène who wears the fur wrap. And if we look carefully, we can see Rubens adjusting her already idealised features in favour of a Venetian version of a classical goddess. The alterations are subtle and not easy to isolate, though we can see that the chin is rounded, the eyes are enlarged and the spacing widened. The hair is longer and disarranged, divorced from associations with contemporary fashion. The eyebrows have new emphasis and are smoothed into a Titianesque crescent. The ribbon around her head, a kind of seventeenth-century 'vamp-band', and the tension of the ear-rings, hint at an exciting exoticism. The inviting smile has evaporated, to be replaced by a far more enigmatic and less focused gaze. This is a deliberately ambiguous picture. The hand on breast – that traditional classical gesture of modesty – has become instead one of exposure. By subtle, indefinable means, Rubens manages to hold our attention exactly half-way between the woman and the woman transformed into the subject of a picture.

The *Hélène Fourment in a Fur Wrap* is Rubens' credo. It illustrates his belief in art addressed to the senses, his method of working from objects rather than ideas. In 1625, when Rubens was working on his Marie de' Medici cycle, he needed models for the sirens who appear in the foreground of the Queen's disembarkation (Plate 18). He wrote to a friend asking him to book the services of three sisters who lived in Brussels. He claimed that he needed these three in particular because of their beautiful bodies, expressive faces and magnificent black hair. Most seventeenth-century painters would have worked up three figures from one model.

This picture is an exceptional example of Rubens' art, and it soars above the normally very high standard of his autograph work. Here he paints tenderly, softly, almost tentatively, with a touch that is less fluent, less premeditated or schematized than in many of his mythological paintings of nudes. On this occasion Hélène does not have to accept the apple from Paris or, disguised as a Sabine, struggle with a Roman soldier. She just has to stand still and let herself become the subject. This is Rubens expressing beauty in art through the object that he felt was most beautiful in life. Looking at Hélène Fourment, draped in furs, we can sense that Rubens could never have made art out of the accidental, that – unlike Rembrandt – he could never have painted models resting from the pose or found beauty in what was, and is, conventionally ugly.

The landscapes

It is not easy to find out how contemporaries reacted to Rubens' landscapes, since he seems to have kept most of them to himself. Even when we can identify a patron it is not particularly helpful for Rubens was never a landscape specialist, producing pictures to order, but an artist who tackled the subject sporadically, emotionally, and primarily for his own pleasure. The Dresden *Boar Hunt* (Plate 12) bought by the Duke of Buckingham in 1627, was originally painted for the large hall in Rubens' own Antwerp house. It is not known whether the pair of small landscapes of a *Morning* and *Evening*, also at York House, were specially commissioned by the Duke, but they are important for they show that Rubens was producing 'Times of the Day' landscapes in the 1620s. The trend away from paintings celebrating seasonal activities towards the rendering of specific light effects, the identification of subjects by light rather than labour, is general in the first half of the seventeenth century. This change had been pioneered by Rubens' acquaintance Adam Elsheimer, whose small painting on copper representing the dawn was famous in Rome. It is significant that Edward Norgate, writing on miniature painting in the 1640s, should state quite dogmatically 'the best and most pleasing kind of landscapes are those representing the morning and evening. For a rising or setting sun affords such variety and beauty of colours . . . for cloudy skies and menacing weather take up as much time as the other, yet are nothing so pleasant'.

Norgate's taste had been formed on Rubens' work, which included storms, but what he says does seem to have a real connection with landscape painting generally in the 1630s when, simultaneously in Italy and in Northern Europe, landscape began to look less obviously composed and dramatic. Artists began to paint the sun. Caravaggio's tonality, so long associated with night scenes, is on the way out and Rubens tries to match the brightness of real daylight with strong directional painting, using bright colour and pigments which are very different from each other in texture. In the 1630s, more gradually and using a very different technique, Claude paints the sun reflected in the sea. At the same time artists began to paint from nature; and we find Rubens making coloured chalk sketches and painting on small wooden panels out of doors. He told Edward Norgate that he had painted his dawn landscape from nature but had 'adjusted it a little'. In the London *Rainbow Landscape* (Plate 41), he celebrates the triumph of his new tonality. A peasant woman lifts a brass ewer against the corn, gold glows against gold, and yet the spatial definition is precise and perfect. At the beginning of the century artists had assembled their landscapes from stylised black and white drawings and motives drawn from older engravings. Conventions of stylisation were so strong that the critic Van Mander jokingly claimed that the real stunted Netherlandish trees had begun to grow exactly like those in contemporary paintings. Landscape then had a very fragile contact with real nature and Rubens' great originality lay in his effort to preserve an account of what it is like to be, and to see colour, out of doors. The sunlit pictures of the 1630s, Claude's harbour scenes, Rubens' sunset meadows, cannot be explained away by any revolution in public taste. They depend on a gradual accumulation of skill on the part of artists, and a gradual elimination of artificial props needed to sustain the perspective illusion. It is even possible that as construction became less difficult and less obvious, subject matter became correspondingly less dramatic and the usual rather than the exceptional in nature became a more frequent theme for landscape painters.

At first Rubens accepted the early seventeenth-century view that landscape was an area for specialists. It was felt that an elaborately developed landscape, packed with botanical and zoological detail, gave the patron a splendid visual bonus. Rubens' *Adam and Eve* (The Hague, Mauritshuis) with its landscape by Jan Bruegel was painted on this assumption at a time when Rubens was ambitious and out to attract influential patrons. In recommending his *Abraham dismissing Hagar* to Sir Dudley Carleton in 1618, Rubens tells him that he has engaged an expert to paint in the landscape 'solely to augment your Excellency's pleasure'. 'Pleasure' is the key word here; and some seventeenth-century theorists, like Rubens' admirer Roger de Piles, believed that landscapes were not only pleasant to look at, but equally pleasant and relaxing to paint. At this time landscapes still had no coherent theory, its propagandists were Northerners and it came low in the hierarchy of the genres. It was not considered so useful as a portrait nor so edifying as an altarpiece; but in practice it was a popular and expanding area. The unofficial upgrading of this genre lay not in developments in seventeenth-century art theory, which were tightly bound up with moral preoccupations, but in the sheer brilliance of the contribution made by great artists: Annibale Carracci, Domenichino, Claude and Rubens himself.

Of all seventeenth-century landscape painting, Rubens' work alone gives us the temporary illusion of being outside. His landscapes are hard to write about, for the principles on which they are constructed are not particularly obvious or predictable. Rubens was not a specialist and his landscapes are not so inbred as those painted by Claude. He does not refine his ideas gradually from picture to picture but by a series of remarkable leaps and bounds brings us into an area not developed further until the nineteenth century. The *Château de Steen* (Plates 37, 38 and 40) and the *Rainbow Landscape* revolve around rather ordinary objects, wattle fences, cows, haystacks and milkmaids, a horse and cart, a huntsman and his dog, the whole paraphernalia of rural domesticity. Rubens' late landscapes are much more than just a tribute to the natural scene: they are frankly triumphal, a celebration of Rubens' own control over the complexity and abundant variety of nature.

As we look at these extraordinary paintings, we can sense an artist working for himself, feeling his way around countryside in which he lived and knew well. Unlike most contemporary landscape painters, Rubens saw brilliant colour in details as well as in larger parts; and for him nature was always in movement, filled with conflicting directions. He aims to share with us the excitement of an exploration and he gives us more to look at per square inch than any other landscapist. He is not inviting us to rest our eyes and minds, with soothing passages of scenery; but teaching us how to see. Placed beside the work of his contemporaries, Rubens' landscapes look almost under-composed, the constructional element being revealed in the ripple of the brush-strokes rather than through the selection of motives. Rubens early landscapes reveal his deep familiarity with the work of local Antwerp painters like Jan Bruegel and Gillis van Coninxloo. His woodland paintings, even the backgrounds of subject pictures like *The Boar Hunt* (Plate 12), have the same heaped-up rhythmic quality, the same exaggeration of the 'accidental' in nature. Rubens responded to the density of their detail and went out with a sketchbook to make his own glossary of nature, his own studies of fallen trees and blackberry bushes.

Armed with this accumulation of detail, he achieved – almost accidentally – a comparable, though less forced, mood of menace. Rubens collected northern landscapes, and sincerely admired specialist skill, but he was cut off from other painters by one important fact: he was unable to think or to draw in straight lines. He leads us into his landscapes through sequences of intersecting wedges, forcing us to approach diagonally and not allowing our eyes that gentle horizontal scanning, from one side to the other and back again, that is so relaxing in the work of Claude, and which is a feature of so much seventeenth-century landscape painting. Rubens is reluctant to put a frame around his landscapes, and his motives are not arranged with the edges of the painting constantly in mind. Trees near the edge will lean out of the picture rather than into it; his figures, likewise, walk in and out of the space that he has created for them. His work can make even a Ruisdael or a Claude look flat.

Rubens plays down the division between ground and sky. His landscapes do not reveal a tasteful selection of dominant vertical forms placed against a light sky. In fact, the tonality of his landscapes does not depend on the colour modulations of the sky as do the paintings of the great Dutch specialists like Ruisdael. With Rubens, light is not merely diffused, it is not soaked up into the weave of a canvas, but is often given a vibrant, positive direction. In the Wallace Collection *Rainbow Landscape*, a shaft of light shines into the picture from the front, suggesting to us that the landscape space begins before it actually appears in the painting. Rubens will pull storm light down from the sky by dragging a coarse brush over the wet ground paint of his panels. It is obvious why Rubens avoids a dominating horizon line; it would have stilled his picture and cancelled out his vision of nature as growing and changing and in perpetual conflict. Unlike most of his contemporaries, Rubens was deeply interested in describing the outside edges of objects seen out of doors. When his French friend Peiresc wrote asking him for an essay on colour, Rubens confessed that it was not colour that he found difficult but contour. Rubens would always extract the maximum life and movement from his contours. The cows in the *Rainbow Landscape* have haloes of silver light, and flashes of scarlet underline their udders. Yellow light will pile up thickly against the outline of twisted tree trunks. Rubens left his technical methods deliberately exposed, realising that a sense of speedy execution can help to create the impression of nature glimpsed, so to say, in passing. Constable, who learnt more from Rubens than from any other painter, was right when he pointed out that the rainbow was the clue to Rubens' attitude towards nature. The rainbow concentrates light revealed as colour and it symbolises a scarcely resolved conflict between storm and sunlight. It is the essence of the spectacular and of what is unstable – and it is, of course, a curve with an arc that breaks the tranquil area of the sky. Its colour can be spread over a landscape, either naturally by reflection, or by calculation, with the colours repeated in the clothing of the peasants in the fields below.

In Rubens' landscapes no holds are barred. He will even attract real light into his picture. It will hit the three-dimensional red berries in the foreground of the *Château de Steen* or the curled edge of a water-lily leaf in the *Rainbow Landscape*. Even in the fragile area of atmospheric perspective he will prefer an almost incongruous solidity, painting the sun as a lump of burnished impasto. In the *Moonlight Landscape* (London, Seilern Collection) the stars have all the literalness of a quattrocento ceiling, they are raised points of white paint. Rubens will try to make tangible even the intangible. In the *Sunset Landscape* (Plate 46) the sun slices the horizon; its light is not purely space creating for it exists in its own right as an object in space. Rubens' recession always depends heavily on the scale of his trees and bushes. He is reluctant to 'fade out' and in *The*

Watering Place (London, National Gallery) minute trees on the skyline are accentuated by being framed in the forked trunk of a foreground tree. Even in Rubens' late landscapes, with their softer painting and creamier colours, we are granted supernatural sight, we see further than we should and hover in a visionary position above the foreground. In finished pictures, Rubens was never quite able to abandon the old sixteenth-century ideal of a world landscape.

It is not easy to define the difference between Rubens' early and late landscapes. The late works have a new lyricism and an increased softness. Recession depends less on the alignment of objects and more on the direction of the brush-strokes. In his early work we might feel that Rubens was imposing on landscape an idea of energy that he had first elaborated in figure paintings. In the late work trees grow like trees and behave less like the fallen heroes in some mythological work. Space takes on a new importance for the mature Rubens and he begins to set more and more subjects out of doors. The mood and meaning of a subject picture is reinforced by the landscape background. Those flat landscapes – like that in the *Rape of the Daughters of Leucippus* (Plate 15) contrasting in scale and almost irrelevant to the subject – drop out of his work. On his late drawings he writes notes reminding himself to give a figure more space. He is now able to project intimate visions into landscapes. In private fantasies he sees the familiar made strange, knights joust on his own estate and lovers play in meadows before moated castles (Plate 47). Rubens becomes fully reconciled to northern art and his knowledge and feelings about the paintings of Pieter Bruegel enter into a new intimate phase. He finds a new delicacy in Bruegel's work and begins to appreciate the delicacy of his touch, the lightly spotted foliage of his trees. He pays a late tribute to his great sixteenth-century predecessor in the *Kermesse* now in the Louvre (Plate 39). The preliminary drawings for this picture show Rubens deliberately holding down his own rhythms, deliberately striving to build up forms with Bruegel's simple shapes circumscribed by blunt outlines. It is almost as if Rubens, in the 1630s, was trying to destroy the whole concept of a hierarchy of subject matter in painting; the separation between subjects seems to be breaking down in a glorious last release. Landscape is taken towards mythology. Rubens discovers that a certain vagueness in painting can create a very precise yet subjective reaction in the spectator. We can see how far he has travelled if we compare his Cassel *Flight into Egypt* (Plate 8) with the *Moonlight Landscape*. In the first, landscape is a by-product of the subject, and its scale is too small for the figures. We are aware of the idea of flight, of figures moving through space. This is a beautiful painting but the mood is Rubens' only by adoption. It properly belongs to Adam Elsheimer and to a smaller format. Here we can sense Rubens' mind at work, we can see him associating Elsheimer with those dark Caravaggesque tones that dominated Italian painting in the first decade of the century. The angel who guides the donkey is lifted straight out of Caravaggio's *Martyrdom of St. Matthew* (Rome, San Luigi dei Francesi). There is something very fragmented in this effort; the source of the idea intrudes on the subject itself. The Seilern *Moonlight Landscape* began life as a *Rest on the Flight into Egypt*, but Rubens painted the figures out and turned the subject from a Biblical scene into a pure landscape, extending the space by adding to the panel, and by converting the donkey, crucial to the Flight of the Holy Family, into a mere grazing animal. But the idea of rest remains, it is inherent in every form – in the rather slack angles of the trees, in the meandering line of the stream, and in the silhouette against the illuminated water. The young Rubens had been able to create an ideal of energy but not one of repose. His

20

art became mellow and relaxed in character as he began to face the therapeutic implications and properties of landscape art. His work had been constructed upon the achievements of the sixteenth century; he had borrowed easily identifiable motives but he had tended to see the works of art themselves in isolation. He had been conscious of what the paintings of his predecessors looked like, but only perhaps late in life did he come to understand their full effect. Only then did he grasp the projection of a mood and begin to play in that glorious half-way house somewhere between fact and fantasy. No other painter in the seventeenth century was able to direct landscape into such autobiographical channels, just as no other artist of the period made such a public decision to have so private a life.

Outline biography

1577 28 June: Peter Paul Rubens born in Siegen, Westphalia, the youngest son of Jan Rubens, a lawyer, and Maria Pypelinckx. In 1568 his father, a Calvinist sympathiser, had fled from Antwerp to Cologne, where he worked as secretary to Anne of Saxony, the wife of Prince William of Orange. Jan Rubens was imprisoned following the discovery of his affair with the princess and is still under house arrest at Siegen when Peter Paul is born.

1587 His father dies fully reconciled with his wife, who leaves Cologne, where the family had lived for ten years, and returns to Antwerp. Rubens and his elder brother Philip attend Rombart Verdonck's Latin School where Balthasar Moretus, future head of the Plantin Press, is a fellow pupil.

1590 Owing to a shortage of money following his sister's marriage, Rubens begins to train as a page in the household of the Countess of Lalaing, but after a few months persuades his mother to apprentice him to a painter.

1598 Recorded as a Master Painter in the Antwerp Guild of St. Luke after serving with three artists, Tobias Verhaeght, Adam Van Noort and Otto Van Veen.

1600 May: departure for Italy. By June he is in Venice and a month later in Mantua where he is appointed court painter to Duke Vincenzo Gonzaga. October: accompanies his patron to Florence; there sees Marie de' Medici's marriage by proxy to Henry IV of France.

1601 Summer: first visit to Rome.

1603 March: leaves Italy for Madrid, where he presents gifts of paintings and vases sent by Vincenzo to Philip III.

1604 Spring: return to Italy.

1605 November: second visit to Rome. He shares a house in the Via della Croce with Philip Rubens, who is librarian to Cardinal Ascanio Colonna.

1606 Still in Rome, where he suffers a serious attack of pleurisy.

1607 Summer: travels with Vincenzo to Genoa.

1608 While completing his Chiesa Nuova altarpiece in Rome he hears that his mother is dangerously ill. He returns to Antwerp, intending to come back to Italy. His mother dies before his arrival on 19 October.

1609 September: appointed court painter to the Habsburg Regents of the Southern Netherlands, the Archduke Albert and the Archduchess Isabella, at an annual salary of 500 florins. He is allowed to live in Antwerp and is exempted from all obligations to his Guild. 3 October: marriage to Isabella Brant. Her father, Jan Brant, is a prominent Antwerp lawyer and a classical scholar.

1610 Buys land and a house in the centre of Antwerp. On the site he later builds a palatial house and studio.

1613-14 Dean of the Society of Romanists (a group of scholars who had visited Rome and who were interested in classical culture).

1616 First contact with Sir Dudley Carleton, the English Ambassador to The Hague. In the following year he buys Sir Dudley's collection of classical sculpture.

1622 January: first visit to Paris to discuss Marie de' Medici's commission for the decoration of the Long Gallery in the Luxembourg Palace.

1623 First reference to his diplomatic activities. Death of his eldest daughter, Clara Serena, aged 12.

1625 February–June: in Paris completing and installing his pictures for the Long Gallery of the Luxembourg. First meeting with the Duke of Buckingham.

1626 20 June: death of Isabella Brant. She had given Rubens four children but only Albert, born 1514, and Nicholas, born 1618, survived childhood.

1627 July: diplomatic mission to Holland. Rubens is escorted by the German painter Joachim Sandrart. Together they visit several studios in Utrecht and Amsterdam. Sells his classical sculpture to the Duke of Buckingham.

1628 August: leaves for Madrid on a diplomatic mission. During this visit he meets Velazquez.

1629 April: leaves Spain and returns to Brussels via Paris on 13 May. June: departs for London to negotiate successfully for an Anglo-Spanish peace. Visits Cambridge, where he receives an honorary degree.

1630 March: before his departure from London is knighted by Charles I. December: marriage to the 16-year-old Hélène Fourment, daughter of a wealthy Antwerp silk merchant. Five children are to be born of the marriage.

1631 December: secret mission to the Prince of Orange at The Hague. He fails to negotiate a peace.

1632 Spring: asks to be relieved of all diplomatic duties.

1635 November: buys a country estate, Het Steen, at Elewijt.

1640 February: made an honorary member of the Accademia di San Luca in Rome. 30 May: dies in Antwerp and is buried in the family chapel in St. Jacques.

List of plates

1. Portrait of the Marchesa Brigida Spinola-Doria. Canvas (cut down), 152×98 cm. Washington, D.C., National Gallery of Art (Kress Collection).
Painted in 1606. Brigida Spinola, a Genoese noblewoman, was 22 when Rubens painted her in the year of her marriage to Giacomo Massimiliano Doria.

2. The Annunciation. Canvas, 224×200 cm. Vienna, Kunsthistorisches Museum.
Painted, about 1609-10, for the Maison Professe, the headquarters of the Antwerp Jesuits, where it remained until the 18th century. It documents the beginning of Rubens' lifelong association with the Flemish Jesuits. Like many of his generation, Rubens was baptised a Protestant but grew up to be a devout Catholic who attended Mass every morning before painting. He lived near the centres of religious controversy. He frequently illustrated Jesuit theological and scientific books and was well read in both Protestant and Catholic propaganda literature. Rubens certainly knew Ignatius Loyola's *Spiritual Exercises*. Here he is painting for a community trained to visualise Biblical episodes in great detail, and accustomed to meditating on them in solitude and darkness.

3. The Apostle Simon. Panel, 108×84 cm. Madrid, Prado. Painted about 1613.

4. The Toilet of Venus. Panel, 123×96 cm. Vaduz, Liechtenstein Collection.
Painted about 1613. A collector's piece, set within a 16th-century Venetian iconographic tradition. This is a domesticated 'Venus Vanitas'; and a painting in which Rubens has tried to suggest an almost sculptural solidity of form. As usual, he was well aware of how his great predecessors had treated the subject: he made a copy, now in the Thyssen Collection, of Titian's *Venus and Cupid with a Mirror*, either from the version now in Washington, or a variant.

5. Rubens and His Wife, Isabella, in the Honeysuckle Arbour. Canvas, 174×132 cm. Munich, Alte Pinakothek. 1609-10.
Painted 1609-10, this portrait commemorates Rubens' marriage to the 17-year-old Isabella Brant on October 3rd, 1609.

6. The Descent from the Cross. Panel, 114×76 cm. London, Courtauld Institute Galleries.
Probably a preliminary study, done about 1611, for the central panel of *The Descent from the Cross* painted in Antwerp between 1611-14. This modello is of high quality. X-rays have revealed pentimenti in the area of the shroud and the left arm of the Virgin. It could have been submitted to Rubens' patrons for approval before he went ahead on the large scale work.

7. The Assumption of the Virgin. Panel, 102×66 cm. London, Buckingham Palace (reproduced by gracious permission of Her Majesty the Queen).
This is a highly finished modello, done in the period 1611-15. It is fully authenticated by a very detailed engraving produced by Schelte à Bolswert about 1650.

8. The Flight of the Holy Family into Egypt. Panel, 40×53 cm. Cassel, Gemäldegalerie.
In its scale, theme and use of moonlight, this painting of 1614 illustrates Rubens' interest in the work of the German landscape painter, Adam Elsheimer, whom he had met when in Rome. In 1611, the year after Elsheimer's death, Rubens wrote to Johann Faber, a German doctor in Rome, telling him: 'I should like to have that picture on copper (of which you write) of the Flight of Our Lady into Egypt come into the hands of one of my compatriots who might bring it to this country.'
Rubens is here concerned with a contrast between the natural moonlight reflected in the water and the supernatural holy light emanating from Mary and the Child.

9. The Flight of St. Barbara. Panel, 33×46 cm. London, Dulwich College Gallery.
A modello for one of the ceiling panels in the south aisle of St. Charles Borromeo, the Jesuit church in Antwerp, newly built and dedicated by the Bishop of Antwerp in September, 1621. Rubens' paintings were destroyed by a fire in 1728.

10. Head of a Child. Panel, 37×27 cm. Vaduz, Liechtenstein Collection.
Painted about 1617. The sitter has not been identified, but it has been suggested that she might be Rubens' eldest daughter, Clara Serena, who died aged 12 in 1623.

11. A Lioness. Black and yellow chalk, washed white body colour, 30×23 cm. London, British Museum.
This study of about 1614-15 was made in connection with a painting of *Daniel in the Lion's Den* which was once in the Hamilton collection, and has recently been acquired by the National Gallery of Art, Washington, D.C. In 1618 Rubens offered Sir Dudley Carleton, English Ambassador to The Hague, a 'Daniel between many lions done from life, an original entirely by my own hand 600 florins'.

12. The Boar Hunt. Panel, 137×169 cm, Dresden, Gemäldegalerie.
This picture, painted about 1616-18, decorated the large hall in Rubens' Antwerp house. In 1627, he sold it to the Duke of Buckingham, who also owned a *Lion Hunt* by Rubens.

13. The Battle of the Amazons. Canvas, 121×165 cm. Munich, Alte Pinakothek.
Executed about 1618, this picture belonged to Rubens' friend Cornelius van der Geest, an Antwerp merchant and connoisseur who had helped him gain the commission for *The Raising of the Cross* in 1610.

14. Detail of Plate 13.

15. The Rape of the Daughters of Leucippus. Canvas, 222×209 cm. Munich, Alte Pinakothek.
The twins Castor and Pollux, famous for their equestrian skill, abducted the two sisters Phoebe and Hilaria, daughters of the priest Leucippus. They were pursued by Idus and Lynceus, who were engaged to the girls. Castor was killed in the fight that followed and Zeus allowed Pollux to die as well. They were given a place amongst the stars and became the Gemini.
Painted about 1618, the composition is borrowed from a group of fighting horsemen that Rubens had copied from Leonardo's *Battle of Anghiari*.

16. The Farm at Laeken. Panel, 84×126 cm. London, Buckingham Palace (reproduced by gracious permission of Her Majesty the Queen).
Painted about 1618. Rubens often enlarged his landscapes as he worked on them. In this case he added 7 cm. to the left and 12·5 cm. at the top and bottom. The church in the background is a simplified version of the building that existed at Laeken until it was demolished in 1894.

17. Landscape with Philemon and Baucis. Panel, 149 ×209 cm. Vienna, Kunsthistorisches Museum.
Painted about 1625. In the *Metamorphoses*, Book 8, Ovid tells the story of Philemon and Baucis. Jupiter and Mercury visited the earth in disguise. Nobody would give them food or shelter, except this elderly couple who, although poor, offered the gods all that they had. As a reward, they and their cottage were saved from the terrible flood with which the gods punished the inhospitable inhabitants of the country.

18. The Reception of Marie de' Medici at Marseilles, 3 November 1600. Canvas, 394×295 cm. Paris, Louvre.
In 1622, Rubens paid his first visit to Paris to discuss with Marie de' Medici, the Queen Mother, her plans for the decoration of two galleries in the recently completed Luxembourg palace. Rubens was fresh from the Jesuit ceiling decoration and the Queen's adviser, the Abbé St. Ambroise, publicly declared that Rubens was the only artist in Europe capable of completing such a huge assignment, that Italian painters could not do in ten years what Rubens had promised to deliver in four. It was agreed that Rubens should be paid 20,000 crowns. At the end of May 1623 nine of the pictures were ready to go to Paris. The Queen expressed complete satisfaction. In February, 1625, Rubens was in Paris with the remaining 13 pictures; he supervised their hanging and was able to gauge the reactions of the Court. For the first gallery, Rubens had to paint twenty-one pictures - which were to line two long walls - commemorating several rather delicate episodes in the life of the Queen, who was the daughter of Francesco de' Medici, the Grand Duke of Tuscany.

19, 20. The Last Judgement. Panel, 183×119 cm. Munich, Alte Pinakothek.
Executed about 1620. Usually known as the 'Small Last Judgement' to distinguish it from a larger painting by Rubens, which is also in Munich and which was com-missioned in 1616 by the Elector Wilhelm for the Jesuit church at Neuberg.

21. The Lamentation Over the Dead Christ. Panel, 31×27 cm. Berlin-Dahlem, Gemäldegalerie.
Executed about 1612-14.

22. Portrait of Ludovicus Nonnius. Panel, 123×100 cm. London, National Gallery.
Painted about 1627. The sitter was the son of a Portuguese physician and was himself a Doctor of Medicine. He was the author of several Latin books and an expert on Greek islands and classical coins. He belonged to Rubens' circle of humanist friends in Antwerp, and Rubens mentions his books in letters of December 1625, April 1626 and August 1627.

23. 'Le Chapeau de Paille' (a portrait of Susanna Fourment?). Panel, 79×55 cm. London, National Gallery.
Painted about 1625. In 1771, this portrait still belonged to the Lunden family, which was related to Rubens. The sitter is probably Susanna Fourment, Rubens' second wife's elder sister. In 1623 she married Arnold Lunden, Master of the Mint.

24. Ludovicus Nonnius (detail from Plate 22).

25. Hélène Fourment (detail from Plate 28).

26. The Apotheosis of the Duke of Buckingham. Panel, 64×64 cm. London, National Gallery.
A modello, made between 1625 and 1628, in connection with a ceiling painting executed for George Villiers, 1st Duke of Buckingham. The large picture made for the Duke's London residence, York House, on the Strand, was destroyed by fire in 1949.

27. Two Apostles. Panel, 35×42 cm. Capesthorne Hall, Cheshire, Lieut.-Col. Sir Walter Bromley-Davenport.
This study was made for an altarpiece of *The Assumption*, painted in 1627 for the church of the Holy Cross in Augsburg, commissioned by the Imperial Captain of that city, Count Otto Heinrich von Fugger. The altarpiece was painted by Rubens' assistants.

28. Hélène Fourment in Her Wedding Dress. Panel, 162×134 cm. Munich, Alte Pinakothek.
Painted about 1630-32. Rubens married the 16-year-old Hélène Fourment in 1630. Her elder brother had married Isabella Brant's sister. She was the daughter of a prosperous Antwerp silk merchant and brought Rubens a substantial dowry, which included yards of expensive material for her trousseau.

29. Self-Portrait. Canvas, 109×85 cm. Vienna, Kunsthistorisches Museum.
Painted about 1633-35. Rubens' marriage certificate of 1630 describes him as 'Knight Secretary to His Majesty's Privy Council and Gentleman of the Household of Her Serene Highness Princess Isabella'. This is how Rubens, 'the

Prince of Painters', liked to see himself; the self-portrait shows a professional court diplomat, with the sword that his rank entitled him to wear. Rubens never painted himself as an artist.

30. Hélène Fourment in a Fur Wrap. Panel, 176×83 cm. Vienna, Kunsthistorisches Museum.
Painted about 1638.

31. Detail of Plate 16.

32. Bacchanal (copy after Titian's painting of *The Andrians*). Canvas, 199×215 cm. Stockholm, National-museum.
Executed about 1636-38, this is a free copy of one of the three mythological paintings made by Titian for Alfonso d'Este between 1518-23. When Rubens was in Rome these pictures were on exhibition in the Aldobrandini Collection.

33. The Rape of the Sabines. Panel, 170×234 cm. London, National Gallery.
Executed about 1635.

34. The Anger of Neptune ('Quos ego'). Panel, 49×64 cm. Cambridge, Mass., Fogg Art Museum.
Painted in 1635.

35. The Rape of Hippodameia. Panel, 26×40 cm. Brussels, Musée des Beaux-Arts.
Executed about 1636-38.

36. St. Ildefonso Receiving the Chasuble from the Virgin (central panel of the Ildefonso Altarpiece). 353×236 cm. Vienna, Kunsthistorisches Museum.
Painted 1630-32. St. Ildefonso was a 7th-century Archbishop of Toledo who wrote a defence of the doctrine of the Immaculate Conception. He fasted for 3 days before the Feast of the Assumption and on that day he entered his church and saw the Virgin Mary seated in the choir stall amid streams of unearthly light. The choir stall was filled with saints singing psalms in her praise. In gratitude for his defence, the Virgin presented him with a specially embroidered chasuble.

37. Detail of Plate 38.

38. Landscape with the Château de Steen. Panel, 137×235 cm. London, National Gallery.
Painted after 1635, this landscape includes an idealised view of Rubens' country house and estate, the Château de Steen, which was situated between Brussels and Malines, and which he bought in 1635. Rubens' son, Albert, told Roger de Piles that his father acquired the house so that he could paint in peace and study landscape. This highly finished picture was painted for Rubens' own pleasure and in 1645 Albert who had been left one half of the actual château bought it out of his father's estate for the large sum of 1,250 gilders.

39. 'La Kermesse Flamande'. Panel, 149×260 cm. Paris, Louvre.
Painted in the first half of the 1630s. In this work we see

Rubens trying to paint a typical Bruegel subject again from nature.

40. Detail of Plate 38.

41. (*a*) *and* (*b*) **Landscape with a Rainbow** (and detail). Panel, 135×234 cm. London, The Wallace Collection.
Painted after 1635.

42. The Meeting of Abraham and Melchizedek. Panel, 66×83 cm. Washington, D.C., National Gallery of Art.
Executed 1627-28. A sketch for one of a series of seventeen tapestries, commissioned by the Archduchess Isabella, and illustrating the doctrine of the Eucharist. They were woven for the Convent of the Barefooted Carmelite nuns in Madrid.

43. Hercules and Minerva Fighting Mars. Watercolour over black chalk, on light brown paper, 37×54 cm. Paris, Louvre, Cabinet des Dessins.
Executed about 1635-37, this is one of several allegorical compositions in which Rubens, after retiring from his diplomatic career, expresses his hatred of war and takes a pessimistic view of European politics.

44. Bathsheba Receiving the Letter from King David. Panel, 167×125 cm. Dresden, Gemäldegalerie.
An illustration of *Samuel* 2, Chapter 11. Bathsheba was the beautiful wife of Uriah, a Hittite captain. While walking on the roof of the palace, King David caught sight of her bathing. He sent for her, and made love to her, and engineered her husband's death in a battle.
Rubens apparently painted this subject only once. The picture, executed about 1636-38, is listed in the inventory of his collection, where it might well have formed an Old Testament companion-piece to *Hélène Fourment in a Fur Wrap* (Plate 30).

45. Portrait of Hélène Fourment with Two of Her Children. Panel, 113×82 cm. Paris, Louvre.
This picture, executed about 1636-37, is unfinished. The children are Clara Johanna (born January 1632) and Frans (born July 1633).

46. Landscape with a sunset. Panel, 48×83 cm. London, National Gallery.
A private work, painted by Rubens for his own pleasure. It must date from after 1635.

47. Landscape with Figures. Panel, 53×98 cm. Vienna, Kunsthistorisches Museum.
Executed after 1635. In the 1630s, Rubens made several paintings of 'Gardens of Love', experiments in high class genre at the opposite end of the scale from 'low life' scenes of peasant merry-making (such as Plate 39).

48. The Three Graces (detail). Panel, 221×180 cm. Madrid, Prado.
Painted in the second half of the 1630s. *The Three Graces* was still in Rubens' possession at the time of his death; and the picture was bought from his estate by Philip IV of Spain.

1. PORTRAIT OF THE MARCHESA BRIGIDA SPINOLA-DORIA. 1606. Washington, D.C.,
National Gallery of Art (Samuel H. Kress Collection)

2. THE ANNUNCIATION. About 1609-10. Vienna, Kunsthistorisches Museum

3. THE APOSTLE SIMON. About 1613. Madrid, Prado

4. THE TOILET OF VENUS. About 1613. Vaduz, Liechtenstein Collection

5. RUBENS AND HIS WIFE, ISABELLA, IN THE HONEYSUCKLE ARBOUR. 1609-10. Munich, Alte Pinakothek

6. THE DESCENT FROM THE CROSS. About 1611. London, Courtauld Institute Galleries

7. THE ASSUMPTION OF THE VIRGIN. 1611-15. London, Buckingham Palace
(reproduced by gracious permission of Her Majesty the Queen)

8. THE FLIGHT OF THE HOLY FAMILY INTO EGYPT. 1614. Cassel, Gemäldegalerie

9. THE FLIGHT OF ST. BARBARA. About 1620. London, Dulwich College Gallery

10. HEAD OF A CHILD. About 1617. Vaduz, Liechtenstein Collection

11. A LIONESS. About 1614-15. London, British Museum

13. THE BATTLE OF THE AMAZONS. About 1618. Munich, Alte Pinakothek

15.   THE RAPE OF THE DAUGHTERS OF LEUCIPPUS. About 1618. Munich, Alte Pinakothek

14.   Detail from THE BATTLE OF THE AMAZONS (*see Plate* 13)

16. THE FARM AT LAEKEN. About 1618. London, Buckingham Palace (reproduced by gracious permission of Her Majesty the Queen)

17. LANDSCAPE WITH PHILEMON AND BAUCIS. About 1625. Vienna, Kunsthistorisches Museum

18. THE RECEPTION OF MARIE DE' MEDICI AT MARSEILLES, 3 NOVEMBER 1600. 1622-25. Paris, Louvre

19. THE LAST JUDGEMENT. About 1620. Munich, Alte Pinakothek

20. Detail from THE LAST JUDGEMENT (*see Plate* 19)

21. THE LAMENTATION OVER THE DEAD CHRIST. About 1612-14. Berlin-Dahlem, Gemäldegalerie

22. PORTRAIT OF LUDOVICUS NONNIUS. About 1627. London, National Gallery

23. 'LE CHAPEAU DE PAILLE' (a portrait of Susanna Fourment?). About 1625. London, National Gallery

24. LUDOVICUS NONNIUS (*detail from Plate 22*)

25. HÉLÈNE FOURMENT (*detail from Plate* 28)

26. THE APOTHEOSIS OF THE DUKE OF BUCKINGHAM. 1625-28. London, National Gallery

27. TWO APOSTLES. About 1627. Capesthorne Hall, Cheshire, Lieutenant-Colonel Sir Walter Bromley-Davenport

28. HÉLÈNE FOURMENT IN HER WEDDING DRESS. 1630-32. Munich, Alte Pinakothek

29.   SELF-PORTRAIT. About 1633-35. Vienna, Kunsthistorisches Museum

30. HÉLÈNE FOURMENT
IN A FUR WRAP.
About 1638. Vienna,
Kunsthistorisches Museum

31. Detail from THE FARM
AT LAEKEN (*see Plate* 16)

32. BACCHANAL
(copy after Titian).
About 1636-38.
Stockholm,
Nationalmuseum

33. THE RAPE OF
THE SABINES.
About 1635.
London,
National Gallery

34. THE ANGER OF NEPTUNE ('Quos Ego'). 1635. Cambridge, Mass., Fogg Art Museum

35. THE RAPE OF HIPPODAMEIA. About 1636-38. Brussels, Musée des Beaux-Arts

36. ST. ILDEFONSO RECEIVING THE CHASUBLE FROM THE VIRGIN (central panel of the
Ildefonso Altarpiece). 1630-32. Vienna, Kunsthistorisches Museum

37. Detail from LANDSCAPE WITH THE CHÂTEAU DE STEEN (*see Plate* 38)

38. LANDSCAPE WITH THE CHÂTEAU DE STEEN. After 1635. London, National Gallery

39. 'LA KERMESSE FLAMANDE'. 1630-35. Paris, Louvre

40. Detail from LANDSCAPE WITH THE CHÂTEAU DE STEEN (*see Plate* 38)

41(*a*) *and* (*b*). LANDSCAPE WITH A RAINBOW (and detail).
After 1635. London, The Wallace Collection

42. THE MEETING OF ABRAHAM AND MELCHIZEDEK. 1627-28. Washington, D.C., National Gallery of Art

43. HERCULES AND MINERVA FIGHTING MARS. About 1635-37. Paris, Louvre, Cabinet des Dessins

44. BATHSHEBA RECEIVING THE LETTER FROM KING DAVID. About 1636-38. Dresden, Gemäldegalerie

45.   PORTRAIT OF HÉLÈNE FOURMENT WITH TWO OF HER CHILDREN. About 1636-37. Paris, Louvre

46. LANDSCAPE WITH A SUNSET. After 1635. London, National Gallery

47. LANDSCAPE WITH FIGURES. After 1635. Vienna, Kunsthistorisches Museum

48. THE THREE GRACES (detail). About 1636-40. Madrid, Prado